FOR

I THINK YOU'D ENJOY THIS BOOK BECAUSE

FROM

PRINCIPLES FOR THE NEXT CENTURY OF WORK

Sense & Respond Press publishes short, beautiful, actionable books on topics related to innovation, digital transformation, product management, and design. Our readers are smart, busy, practical innovators. Our authors are experts working in the fields they write about.

The goal of every book in our series is to solve a real-world problem for our readers. Whether that be understanding a complex and emerging topic, or something as concrete (and difficult) as hiring innovation leaders, our books help working professionals get better at their jobs, quickly.

Jeff Gothelf & Josh Seiden

Series co-editors **Jeff Gothelf** and **Josh Seiden** wrote *Lean UX* (O'Reilly) and *Sense & Respond* (Harvard Business Review Press) together. They were co-founding principals of Neo Innovation (sold to Pivotal Labs) in New York City and helped build it into one of the most recognized brands in modern product strategy, development, and design. In 2017 they were short-listed for the Thinkers50 award for their contributions to innovation leadership. Learn more about Jeff and Josh at www.jeffgothelf.com and www.joshseiden.com.

The Government Fix
How to innovate in government
Hana Schank & Sara Hudson

Outcomes Over Output
Why customer behavior is the key metric for business success
Josh Seiden

OKRs at the Center
How to use goals to drive ongoing change and
create the organization you want
Natalia Hellesoe & Sonja Mewes

What Do We Do Now?
A product manager's guide to strategy in the time of crisis
Randy Silver

Ethical Product Development
Practical techniques to apply across
the product development life cycle
Pavini Reddy

Hiring Product Managers
Using Product EQ to go beyond culture and skills
Kate Leto

The Culture Project
30 days to reboot your organization
Thomas Bradbury

To keep up with new releases or submit book ideas to the press,
check out our website at www.senseandrespondpress.com.

A CULTURE
OF SAFETY

Issued in print and electronic formats.
ISBN 979-8-9852402-0-7 (paperback).
ISBN 979-8-9852402-1-4 (ebook).

Editor: Victoria Olsen
Designer: Mimi O Chun
Interior typesetting: Jennifer Blais

Published in the United States by Sense & Respond Press
www.senseandrespondpress.com

Printed and bound in the United States.
1 2 3 4   23 22 21 20

Alla Weinberg

A CULTURE OF SAFETY

Building a work environment where people can think, collaborate, and innovate

SENSE &
RESPOND
PRESS

For my husband, Josh.

Your plan is working my love.

INTRODUCTION

I woke up late one Friday morning, feeling both satisfied and exhausted after having facilitated an intense multi-day training session that ended the previous day. Still in bed, I picked up my phone and took a quick glance at my email when I noticed one from a teammate titled "My feedback." Being an introvert, I usually need several days to process any event before I can provide feedback, so I was surprised that my colleague was able to reflect so quickly.

Curious to hear his, hopefully glowing, thoughts, I opened the email and found that it was actually a copy of an email he sent to my manager—about all the things that I did wrong at the event; he quoted specific phrases I said when I was trying to collaborate and make decisions, as examples of my poor performance.

In that moment, I noticed my heart beating out of my chest, I felt light-headed, and hot. I experienced a mix of emotions: anger, hurt, and sadness. My mind began to race, "What will happen to me? Am I going to get fired?" My trust in him plummeted to zero, as I read over and over again my own words used against me. The same words I used to share my thoughts and ideas when I felt safe to work with him.

I put the phone down to avoid the temptation of sending off a heated reply, and began strategizing ways to avoid working with him in the future and having as little interaction with him as possible. I no longer felt safe collaborating with a teammate because I didn't know if my thoughts will be held against me later.

This experience is just one example of the many ways that safety gets compromised at work. A few other examples include:

» Backlash for pointing out or reporting mistreatment
» Telling someone they "shouldn't feel" a certain way
» Criticizing or dismissing ideas by labeling them "stupid" or "irrelevant."

When safety is compromised, people begin to protect themselves by holding back ideas, feelings, and thoughts. They create relationship workarounds, which take up a lot of emotional and mental energy that could be used toward learning, building, and innovating the business.

In some cases the impact can be disastrous, such as with the catastrophic failure of the Boeing 737 Max jets that led to two fatal crashes in 2018 and 2019, the firing of the CEO, and indefinite grounding of the jets. The failure of the jet has in part been attributed to the lack of a culture of safety at the company, where employees knew what was wrong with both the design of the jet and the project management but did not feel safe enough to speak up.

In other cases, a lack of innovation is difficult to see because it's not a big failure that jumps out at you. But over time, a company becomes less relevant and less vital in the marketplace because it didn't innovate. In today's market, irrelevance can happen rather quickly, such as when Netflix put Blockbuster completely out of business in just six years.

Most leaders recognize that today's business challenges are complex, and can be solved only by people working well together. An organization that doesn't have a culture of safety—a culture in which people face microaggressions, withhold emotions, avoid conflict, stay silent, shy away from risks—will not only be unable to address complexity, but will also lack the agility to respond to the constant changes business face every day.

Sitting at the intersection of product design and people development, and having had many experiences similar to the one I described above, I feel a personal sense of urgency to arm leaders with practical tools—not more theories—to help create cultures of safety. Personally, I want to help leaders create the type of work environments where I want to work.

As you read and practice the tools provided in this book, please keep in mind that a culture of safety is not a destination. You do not ever arrive at a culture of safety, check that box, and move on to other things. Creating a culture of safety is an ongoing process that requires regular attention and effort, and fundamentally, changing how you think about work.

CHAPTER 1: WHY SAFETY?

Without safety, we literally cannot think. Why is this the case? The truth is that although our external environment has changed dramatically, our brains have not evolved that much in the last 10,000 years; they are still designed to detect and protect us from threats to our survival.

Although threats no longer show up as predators waiting to eat us, we do face both physical and psychological threats in our lives all the time, a few examples:

» An angry message from a client or stakeholder
» The diagnosis of an unexpected illness
» Losing a great team member
» Yet another company reorganization
» Missing a target or deadline
» A new leader joining the team
» A car barreling toward you as you step into the street
» Giving an important presentation.

While the brain has deep interconnections and cross-connections among all its different regions, threats to our survival are processed in a very specific sequence.

First, external input from our five senses and information from our body is transmitted up the brainstem to the primitive brain, where it is checked for a threat. It does not matter if the threat is real or imagined; the primitive brain understands only survival and protection. It loves whatever it feels will keep us safe, and fears and hates whatever it feels will do us harm. As soon as that region of our brain detects a threat—without any ability to discern between a hungry lion and an angry stakeholder—it begins the carefully orchestrated yet near-instantaneous sequence of hormonal changes and physiological responses that helps us to deal with the threat. The hormones cortisol and adrenaline are released, as our body prepares to fight, flight, freeze, or faint. These are the only commands the primitive brain knows and the only choices it is able to make.

Physically, we may experience a racing heart, heat in the face or body, light-headedness, tightness in the chest, shallow breathing, and sweaty palms. According to research, all of these changes happen so quickly that people usually aren't aware of them. In fact, the wiring is so efficient that the brain starts the hormonal cascade even before the visual centers have had a chance to fully process what is happening. That's why people are able to jump out of the path of an oncoming car even before they see it.

So our primitive brain certainly has its benefits!

Next, the information passes from our primitive brain to our mammalian brain, which is in charge of our emotional responses. We might feel scared and then relieved to have been able to jump out of the way of that oncoming car.

Lastly, the information enters the rational brain, which is in charge of language, thought, reasoning, and analysis. This is the part of our brain that we use for thinking. Our thinking mind is third in line after our primitive and mammalian brains. That's why when we put a hand on a hot frying pan, the hand jerks away instantly, while our thinking brain goes, "What just happened? *Ow!*"

Here is the interesting part, the primitive brain is strong enough to override our thinking brain whenever it senses real or imagined danger. If the primitive brain registers a threat, our rational brain quiets down and our operating IQ drops to between 50 and 70 points. This is half of the operating IQ when we are in a calm state, which is between 100 and 120.

Half.

So when we are in survival mode, we no longer have the ability to think, collaborate, or be creative. In this state, we do not have the capacity to handle complex situations or make good decisions.

And, according to the Cynefin (pronounced ku-NEV-in) model, created by David Snowden and Mary E. Boone, complex issues are much more prevalent in the business world than most leaders realize. They define complex situations as ones in which outcomes cannot be accurately predicted regardless of the level of expertise or effort invested in the solution. A few examples of complex situations include:

- » Going through a digital transformation
- » Adopting an agile development process
- » Investing in a new product line or market
- » Shifting to a new company culture
- » Moving from an on-site to a remote workforce.

And even beyond these complex situations, organizations today are also facing "the unknowables" or chaotic situations such as terrorism, social upheaval, climate disasters, and pandemics.

Now, consider the impact of neurology on our ability to respond to complex and chaotic situations. It's huge. When our operating IQ plummets, so does our ability to do our job, make good decisions, work effectively with others, create value for customers, and even help our organization to survive.

Even with the most talented, knowledgeable, and skilled people, without a safe work environment, people literally cannot contribute what they know when it's needed the most.

Although no one can control the activation of the primitive brain, we can create environments in which the likelihood of such a response is significantly lower and people are equipped to regulate themselves back to a normal state.

We do this by building and maintaining a culture of safety.

WHAT IS SAFETY?

In this book, when I am talking about safety—the type of safety that allows people to think, collaborate, and innovate, I am referring to three types of safety:

1. **Physical Safety:** the shared belief that everybody is valued, respected, and included.

2. **Emotional Safety:** the shared belief that all emotions are valid and the expression of any emotion is welcome.

3. **Psychological Safety:** the shared belief that no one on the team will embarrass or punish anyone else for admitting a mistake, asking a question, or offering a new idea.

The three types of safety map to the primitive brain, the mammalian brain, and the rational brain, respectively. When people are safe in these three ways, they can operate at the highest IQ and are capable of analytical thinking, creative insight, and collaborative problem-solving.

What is important to notice about all three types of safety is that they are all created in relationship with others. When we feel connected and secure in our interpersonal relationships, our nervous system can relax, allowing us access to our intelligence. This makes sense from a biological standpoint because we are hardwired to belong to a tribe that can protect us from outside threats.

Unfortunately, most of us don't feel a sense of safety in our work tribes. The symptoms that indicate weak and unsafe work relationships show up as follows:

» People don't ask many questions during meetings.
» People don't feel comfortable owning up to mistakes or place blame on others when mistakes are made.

» The team avoids difficult conversations and hot-button topics.

» Executives and team leaders tend to dominate meeting discussions.

» People don't often venture outside of their job descriptions to support other teammates.

» People don't ask one another for help when they need it.

» There are hardly any disagreements or differing points of view.

» People don't know one another personally, just professionally.

When our internal work relationships don't feel safe, we spend our time and energy protecting ourselves from one another instead of learning, collaborating, and responding to external changes.

The tools and practices presented in this book for creating a culture of safety are focused on strengthening interpersonal relationships with safety as the outcome of those relationships.

SAFETY REFLECTION

As a leader, it's important to take a moment to reflect on times when you have felt safe within a group and what made you feel safe. As every airplane safety briefing says, we need to put on our own oxygen mask first before helping anyone else. As a leader, you need to increase the safety of your relationships first, before you can help your organization.

STEP 1

Scan back in your memory and think of a time when you felt really safe with a group of people. It could be a group at work; a group from school or volunteer organization; a sports team; a music group—even your family or friends.

Take a few minutes to bring yourself back to that time and those people, think about what you accomplished together and even what you might have had to overcome.

STEP 2

Consider and capture your answers to this question: What attributes made that group safe?

STEP 3

Think about three to five people who are most critical to your success at work. Include your peers, direct reports, your manager, any skip-levels or executives, and any key external vendors or others.

For each relationship, reflect on the following questions:
» What safety attributes, that you wrote down in Step 2, are present for you in this relationship?
» What safety attributes, that you wrote down in Step 2, are missing for you in this relationship?
» Do you feel more or less safety with specific groups of people such as your peers, reports, executives?

CHAPTER 2: WHAT IS CULTURE?

Culture is one of the most powerful forces on the planet. We can sense its presence in highly effective teams, and we can feel its effects when it's toxic.

Although everyone knows that free lunches and game tables don't make a culture, what leaders don't know is that culture isn't about values either. If company cultures were about values, then more companies would be transparent, collaborative, purposeful, and caring, when frankly they are not.

In her experience working with organizations, University of Houston professor Brené Brown, Ph.D., found that only 10 percent of organizations have operationalized their values into teachable and observable behaviors that are used to hold people accountable.

Only 10 percent.

So just because you have stated values doesn't mean you are going to do anything about them or that they will be reflected in your culture.

This is because culture is an emergent property of the relationships that people have with one another.

What this means is that you can't predict the type of culture your company will have just by looking at individual personality traits or skills. A culture arises out of the way those individuals interact with and relate to one another. This is why certain groups of people add up to be more than the sum of their parts, while others add up to less.

One of my favorite stories that illustrates the idea of culture arising out of relationships comes from retired U.S. Navy Captain David Marquet. Marquet spent a year studying every part of a submarine called the *USS Olympia*, but at the last minute he was reassigned to be the captain of a completely different submarine, the *USS Santa Fe*. This submarine was the worst performing vessel in the fleet and had the lowest sailor reenlistment rate in the Navy, so Marquet knew he would be inheriting a troubled crew. He didn't have any control over the crew that was assigned to the ship or their roles; the only variable Marquet could control was how the crew interacted with him and one another.

The standard interaction in the Navy is that the captain gives good orders and the crew follows the orders. But Marquet didn't know this submarine, so there was no way he could give good orders! So he decided to change the captain-to-crew relationship. He vowed to stop giving orders and instead trust the crew to think and inform him of their intent to do something. So if a sailor wanted to submerge the ship, Marquet wanted them to come to him and say, "I intend to submerge the ship, Captain."

In the beginning, this change was difficult for the crew members who were used to doing what they were told. The biggest obstacle in their way was interpersonal fear: fear of being wrong, of being judged by others, fear of being different. So Marquet made it his job to build safety all day long. He would say things like: "Yes that is ok," or "Express that in probabilities," or "If you were the captain, what would you want to know about that?"

As the crew began to relate differently to Marquet, they also began to relate differently to one another. The crew started communicating more with one another and eventually, every crew member was aware of what was happening on the entire ship, not just at their own station. Marquet built a culture of safety by changing the way he related to the crew.

What was the result? Every single person on Marquet's crew reenlisted, and the *Santa Fe* went from being the Navy's worst-ranking ship to breaking-all-Navy-records first.

So if you want to shape the culture of your team or organization, focus on shifting the relationships between individuals—starting with your relationships first—rather than roles or the individuals themselves.

VISUALIZE THE CULTURE

When leaders I work with want to get a more holistic view of the culture in their organization, they still find the concept of a culture ephemeral and difficult to grasp. So I would like to offer a much more tangible way to think about culture.

One of the quickest ways to make culture more tangible is to think about the culture as a living, breathing, dynamic organism with a life of its own.

You can start by imagining your organizational culture as a creature. See this creature in your mind's eye and notice...

» What does it look like?

» How does it move?

Ask the creature...

» How are you strong?

» What helps you feel safe?

» What advice do you have for me?

» What advice do you have for my organization?

See, hear, sense, or feel the creature's answer.

CHAPTER 3:
THE NATURE OF FEAR

The opposite of safety is fear: a deep-rooted fear
that our basic human needs for safety/security,
connection/love, and control/autonomy will not be
met and we will perish.

The biggest catalyst of that fear is... change. Whether it is changing a work relationship or a culture, our brain is hardwired to be vigilant to any change. In some ways, we are all here today because our ancestors didn't stick around to find out if the rustling in the bushes was a lion or a lizard.

So, changing the way you relate to people and creating a culture of safety is likely to activate a fear response on all three levels. First, the primitive brain will create a physiological response usually experienced as a tightening or tensing of our muscles, then our mammalian brain will set off feelings of fear, and finally our rational brain will focus on critical or negative thoughts about the change.

Perhaps you have already experienced a tightness in your chest, arms, or stomach, feelings of fear, and some critical thoughts such as:

» This won't work in my organization.
» Who am I to create a culture of safety?
» I don't have enough time or resources to change the culture
» Once I get a seat at the table then I will be able to create more safety.

It's natural to feel resistance to change. Change is scary, and on top of that, our brain is working hard to keep us alive by minimizing anything that could lead to change.

And, in order to be able to help yourself and your team build a new culture, you, dear leader, have to first be able to identify and move through your own fears. Then, it's your job to grow your capacity—emotionally expanding in size and volume—the amount of discomfort you can stand so that you can respectfully guide your team through their fears into a new way of working. This is the core work of leadership—to create a calm nervous system within yourself, even in the face of great discomfort, so that you can lead others to settle their nervous systems and have access to their full intelligence.

WHAT IS THE PURPOSE OF FEAR?

To understand the nature of fear is to understand that it's not something that you get rid of, suppress, push through, or avoid, but something that you turn toward, stay with, and invite. In Western culture, we are, ironically, so scared of facing and feeling our fear that we have come up with a euphemism to describe it, we call it "stress." In 2019, the American Institute of Stress reported that 83 percent of people suffer from workplace stress, with 55 percent of Americans reporting experiencing stress during the day.

So what is the fear—that the majority of us are experiencing every day—trying to tell us?

According to Karla McLaren, author of *The Language of Emotions*, every emotion has a purpose and information for you. The purpose of fear, she says, is to give you:

> "the energy and focus you need to orient yourself to change or novel situations. This often means that you have to stop what you're doing, or at least slow down. Unfortunately, most of us fight anything that tries to halt our forward movement—which means that most of us fight our fear. This is a serious mistake with serious consequences."

The main consequence of fighting fear is that it begins to "warm up" your primitive brain to react and you begin responding to people and circumstances around you using primarily unconscious survival strategies such as covert or overt aggression, withdrawal, or resignation. These survival strategies can be mapped to a model called the "Drama Triangle." The Drama Triangle was developed by Stephen Karpman to describe ways that people relate to themselves and each other. Each position in the Drama Triangle exhibits unhealthy—yet common—behaviors or survival strategies that incite conflict, erode safety, and diminish intelligence.

DRAMA TRIANGLE

PERSECUTOR
HUMAN NEEDS: SAFETY/SECURITY
IMPACTS: PHYSICAL SAFETY

RESCUER
HUMAN NEEDS: CONNECTION/LOVE
IMPACTS: EMOTIONAL SAFETY

VICTIM
HUMAN NEEDS: CONTROL/AUTONOMY
IMPACTS: PSYCHOLOGICAL SAFETY

If you are in the Prosecutor position, instead of facing your fear and human need for safety, you would start finding people or circumstances to blame. Blame is a common way to discharge the discomfort of fear and greatly diminishes physical safety. It might show up as blaming yourself, "I should have known better and made a different choice. I should have been a better leader"—or blaming others, "I wouldn't have these problems if it wasn't for them. I was fine until they showed up." You know them: those people who look or think differently and are clearly "underperforming" or those people in that other business unit who didn't do their job. Hello silos!

The leader in the Rescuer position is so busy helping and taking care of other people, that they don't have time to deal with their own fears. This leader will feel a temporary sense of relief by focusing on others instead of on their fears, and even get an emotional boost from being the one with all the answers. Yet, a leader in this position will often avoid delegation, disempower other people by taking on their work, micromanage, and go through cycles of high productivity followed by periods of exhaustion. All in an effort to avoid looking at what is causing their fear and acknowledging their human need for connection. If someone is expressing emotions, you will often hear a Rescuer dismiss those emotions by saying, "You don't need to feel that way, everything is ok" or "It's not that bad, you are overreacting" as a way to suppress their own discomfort. This kind of behavior invalidates other people's feelings and decreases emotional safety.

Finally, a leader in the Victim position feels that everything is happening personally to them. Their circumstances are happening to them, as are external factors like the economy, competitors, time, or even the weather. A leader in this position will feel disempowered and often complain of not having enough: not enough time, money, people, or resources of some kind.

This leader will often fail to protect members of their own team because "there was nothing I could do" and diminish the team's psychological safety by saying things like "this is the way we have always done it" or "that's not feasible here." Some leaders even use gaslighting as a tactic to feel a sense of control. The Victim position is used to shirk responsibility and to suppress the deep fear that the human need for control will not be met.

Each of us will have different starting positions on the Drama Triangle, and may find some positions more comfortable than others. Yet, in each circumstance we will continue to cycle through each of the positions until we can shift out of it. The way to shift out of the Drama Triangle is to destigmatize fear and begin to face it instead.

FEAR INVENTORY

The fear inventory tool will allow you to slow down and increase your capacity to stay with the discomfort of fear. With practice, your capacity to process fear will allow you to focus and help your team move through their fear toward safety. This practice can be done individually or as part of a weekly ritual with a team. The power of this tool lives in the regular practice of writing the inventory, of slowing down and saying hello to fear. Here's how to do it:

1. Set a timer for three minutes.

2. Think of a belief, person, or situation that upsets you, when you felt angry, hurt, sad, or disappointed. Write about this specific topic on a piece of paper.

3. Write down the fears that are associated with that topic using the following format: "I have a fear that I ...."

Examples:
- » I have a fear that I won't be successful.
- » I have a fear that I am not as good as John.
- » I have a fear that I am not valued.
- » I have a fear that I don't like my team.

4. Write in a stream of consciousness for the entire duration of the timer. Do not stop to think or take your pen off the paper. It is OK to repeat yourself as many times as you need.

5. Read aloud your fear inventory to yourself or to someone that you trust.

6. Rip up your inventory.

CHAPTER 4: SHIFT FROM FEAR TO SAFETY

The reason our workplaces are so riddled with fear is that they were originally created to increase efficiency of workers in completing simple, manual tasks.

During the Industrial Revolution, most workers were so poorly educated that Frederick Winslow Taylor, author of *The Principles of Scientific Management*, described the typical laborer as "so stupid that the term *percentage* has no meaning to him." The solution that Taylor proposed, now coined as Taylorism, was to create a caste system of thinkers and doers, whereby management did the thinking and workers carried out the doing. At that time, it was certainly an advantage to companies to maximize the productivity and efficiency of their workers because creating more widgets at lower costs was the primary business model. This is why nowadays, we say we are "doing work" even though much of the work in the knowledge economy is "thinking work."

Sadly, in the time since the Industrial Revolution, the caste system set up by Taylorism has persisted. Although people today are far better educated, the distinction between managers and employees is still deeply entrenched. This is evident in the language that organizations use to measure work, words such as *productivity* and *performance*, pointing to the outdated desire to increase the speed and quantity of work being produced rather than the quality of thought and creativity behind the work. It is no wonder then, that since 2000, the score on the U.S. Gallup poll of employee engagement has not risen above 34 percent. As a result, the vast reservoir of human ingenuity is completely untapped with fewer than one in 10 people reporting that they strongly agree with the statement "I take risks at my job that could lead to new products or solutions."

The primary reason that the Industrial Era caste system has endured throughout the last century is because it is rooted in Taylorist beliefs about people at work. The fear-based beliefs are that people are lazy, dishonest, and in need of direction. According to research conducted by author Frederic Laloux, the beliefs that underpin this worldview include:

» People are lazy; leaders need to motivate them with reward or punishment to ensure performance.
» People work primarily for money; they will do what it takes to make as much money as possible.
» People are selfish; they will put their own interests ahead of the organization.
» People need to be told what to do, how to do it, and when to do it; leaders need to hold them accountable.
» Only leaders are capable of making good decisions that affect the economic performance of the company.
» People do not want to be responsible for their actions or for decisions that affect the economic performance of the company.
» People are like interchangeable parts in a machine. One person with a set of specific skills is pretty much the same as any other person with the same skills.
» Feelings and emotions are not professional, and need to be set aside so work can get done.

These beliefs may sound harsh, yet they are the basis for the structures and practices we have in organizations today. They create environments where shame, blame, judgment, and fear are used to control people's behavior, and have a direct impact on company results.

Let's take a look at some of the most common workplace practices that stem from fear-based beliefs. A company that uses an employee ranking system—which rewards high achievers and punishes underperformers by putting them on a performance improvement plan—holds the belief that people are lazy and leaders need to motivate them with reward or punishment to ensure performance. Tying bonuses and promotions to output or hours spent at the office supports the belief that people work primarily for money and will do what it takes to make as much money as possible. Hierarchical approval processes for budget spending or experimenting with new ideas are common in many organizations, stemming from the belief that only leaders are capable of making good decisions that affect economic performance of a company. Crying in the office is judged as weak and unprofessional, with many people crying in bathroom stalls or alone in their offices. And, policies that have little flexibility about where and when work gets done come from the belief that leaders need to tell people what to do, how to do it, and when to do it.

The beliefs also show up in the way leaders relate to the people they are leading. If a person made a mistake, a fear-based leader might use:

» Guilt: "I'm very disappointed in you."
» Blame: "I thought I could depend on you. You told me you could do it."
» Shame: "You're showing me that you can't be trusted."
» Punitive consequences: "You've left me no choice, I am taking you off this project."

And they work... sort of. They result in compliance, but not in creativity, agility, ingenuity, or safety.

Instead, let's think about ways a safety-based leader might relate to an individual who made a mistake:

» They might share feelings without judgment: "I'm feeling disappointed. I don't think either of us wanted this to happen."
» They could be curious and acknowledge the person: "I'd like to hear what happened. I know you always try to make good choices."

> » They might share their needs: "I wanted you to consider my advice. It helps me when I can rely on you to hear me."
> » They could work to create cooperative solutions: "What would have helped you manage this? Let's think about some new solutions."

So I am here to tell you that a shift from fear to safety is possible, and the fastest way to do it is to shift your beliefs.

Take Bob Chapman, the CEO of Barry-Wehmiller, an equipment manufacturing company as an example. He had a profound shift in his beliefs while attending a wedding. Chapman was sitting in a pew watching the proud father of the bride walk his daughter down the aisle toward the groom. Upon reaching the altar, the bride's father offered his daughter's hand to the groom and then spoke the ceremonial words "Her mother and I give this daughter to be wed." At the moment, Chapman realized the deeper meaning behind those words: "We trust you with our daughter, a most precious human being, and expect through your union you will love her and take great care of her and allow her to grow into all that she was meant to be." This realization created a shift in Chapman and what he believed about the people in his company. In that moment, he began to see that everyone working at the company was someone's precious child entrusted into the company's care, not just an interchangeable part in a machine.

This led to several big changes at Chapman's company: the removal of time clocks and break bells on factory floors; an employee recognition program; investing in coaching and developing the "B players" in the company; and the creation of the guiding principles of leadership, which outlined a new set of beliefs for the company.

ACT AS IF

To shift a belief, which is what we hold to be true about the world, you need to act as if the new belief is already true.

Think about a challenge you are having with your team or organization. Select one of the following new beliefs:

> » People are creative, thoughtful, trustworthy adults capable of making important decisions.
> » Good ideas can come from any person in the company.
> » People are accountable and responsible for their decisions and actions.
> » People are fallible and make mistakes.
> » People are people, not resources, parts, or obstacles.
> » People want to use their talents and skills to make a contribution to the organization.
> » People who are struggling need more support and care, not less.
> » It is natural for people to experience and express emotions.

Ask yourself the following question: "If I believed [the new belief that you just selected], what would I do?"

Then follow through with that action.

The more frequently you ask yourself the question and then follow through with that action, the faster the new belief you have chosen will take root. Soon, you won't have to *act* as if you believe it; you simply will believe it to be true.

CHAPTER 5: WAYS TO BUILD SAFETY

So far, we have covered ways that you as an individual leader can begin to build safety for yourself first—by reflecting on the safety of your work relationships, connecting to the culture of your organization, facing your fears, and shifting your beliefs.

Now, let's talk about practical ways you can build safety for others. It's important to remember that safety is created in the relationships between people, and that it's not possible to make anyone feel safe directly. Instead, you can set up different ways for individuals to relate and interact with one another so that the feeling of safety can emerge.

I have found that meetings are the most powerful mechanism for building safety. Meetings have regularity, a format, and a specific way that people interact with one another. What people choose to discuss and how they talk to one another in those meetings can create more or less safety. So by making modifications to existing meetings, or by creating new ones for specific purposes, you can start building a culture of safety.

In essence: Change your meetings, change your culture.

In the sections below, I will talk in more depth about physical, emotional, and psychological safety and provide ideas for meeting practices that I have seen work to create that specific type of safety.

Based on our neurology, physical safety needs to exist before you can have emotional safety, and emotional safety needs to exist before you can have psychological safety. This means that the people in your organization need to first feel physically safe and then emotionally safe in order to be able to think, collaborate, and innovate.

PHYSICAL SAFETY

I define physical safety as the shared belief that everybody is valued, respected, and included.

Physical safety maps to the primitive brain, which is in charge of our survival. When the primitive brain detects a real or imagined threat to our body, it blocks any information from reaching our rational brain until after it has sent a cascade of hormones with the message to fight, flight, freeze, or faint. If people's bodily experiences in the workplace are not consciously considered, within a manner of milliseconds the brain of those affected will register the physical or virtual work space as dangerous, literally inhibiting their ability to think.

Sadly, aside from ergonomics, people's bodily experiences are rarely considered in modern workplaces. Mostly, the body is seen as the vehicle to move the head around from one meeting room to another. Yet, as our neurology reveals, without a sense of physical safety, our rational brain doesn't even get the opportunity to think.

The lack of physical safety is experienced most acutely by minority groups. People who are not part of the dominant group often feel and experience that their bodily differences will cause them to stand out and be a target for abuse. Abuse can come in the form of microaggressions, backlash to pointing out mistakes or mistreatment, threats to job security, discrimination, or harassment.

The deep fear of physical safety felt most acutely by minority groups often stems from racialized trauma experienced throughout an individual's lifetime in which they were personally threatened with harm or injury, exposed to humiliating or shaming events, or witnessed discrimination of someone else of their race.

Contrary to what many people believe, trauma is not emotional; it is a physical response in the body. According to therapist and trauma specialist, Resmaa Menakem:

> "Our bodies have a form of knowledge that is different from our cognitive brains. The knowledge is typically experienced as a felt sense of constriction or expansion, pain or ease, energy or numbness. Often this knowledge is stored in our bodies as wordless stories about what is safe and what is dangerous."

In the aftermath of traumatic situations, the primitive brain may embed a reflexic trauma response in our bodies, which can get activated easily in the workplace and show up as disordered thinking, difficulty concentrating, anxiety attacks, hopelessness, self-hatred, and even in instances of violence.

So, many people in minority groups work twice as hard to sustain a sense of physical safety, compared to their peers. In the workplace, this looks like "code-switching," which includes embracing the dominant group's behaviors and vernacular at work and switching back to a more authentic self when around friends and family. For example, Black men say it's often part of their job to be careful about their tone of voice so others don't view them as the stereotypical "angry black man"; Black and Latina women frequently report taking pains to speak without an accent or to avoid using slang.

Code-switching becomes more difficult in a virtual environment as people are forced to expose their homes and lifestyles to their colleagues, and potentially come off as "unprofessional." Research conducted by NYU has shown that Black women report "a significant mental strain associated with trying to live up to a professional ideal that was originally created to stifle, rather than support, diversity."

In the United States, the typical picture of the professional ideal is a cisgender white-bodied male. A white male body that has never experienced: someone coming up to them and saying, "I got a tan, we are almost the same color now" as they put their arm next to yours; being asked to smile more so that you come off as less aggressive; people calling you by the wrong pronoun; looking at the executive suite and not seeing anyone that resembles you; or having to take a sick day because your body is in pain from your menstrual cycle.

When people experience fear about their physical safety—when they don't feel that their bodies are valued, respected, and included—they spend precious time and energy finding creative ways to keep themselves safe rather than finding creative ways to solve business problems.

One of the biggest threats to those who are not white males is the threat of job loss. People whose bodies are different from the majority—who stand out—are the most afraid of losing their jobs and financial security. In the body, a job loss is registered as a direct threat to survival because it goes to a person's ability to meet their basic human needs. People who are scared about losing their jobs because their bodies are different will prioritize the work that keeps them safe, rather than taking the risk of being seen, working with another department, or offering a truly novel idea that creates value for the business.

MEETING PRACTICES

The following meeting practices work to begin creating a culture in which people feel that their bodies are valued, respected, and included. Although these practices may feel uncomfortable at first—especially to the dominant group in an organization—when these meetings are held on a regular basis, the discomfort fades and people begin to perceive them as normal.

Body Scan

Purpose: This practice lets each individual connect to and settle in their body. This allows people to be more calm, alert, and fully present. A regular body scan practice conducted as a group helps to build a sense of physical safety between bodies.

Suggested Cadence: At the start of every meeting

Read the following instructions slowly to everyone in the meeting:

» Sit comfortably in a chair.

» Take a few breaths, feeling the temperature and texture of the air as you breathe in and out.

» Close your eyes or focus softly in the distance.

» Notice the chair against your back. Notice the sensation of your feet on the ground.

» Starting with the top of your head, slowly scan your body from top to bottom. Pay attention to each part of your body as you slowly move your attention downward.

» Notice where there is pain or discomfort, where there is tension or constriction, and where there is relaxation.

» First move slowly down your forehead, then through your face, jaw, and down your neck. Notice the sensations in your body.

» Follow your attention as it moves across the top of your shoulders and onto your shoulder blades, then down your torso and into and down your arms. Notice the sensations in your body.

» Continue to descend down your torso and arms and into your hands. Experience your attention spreading into your fingers and then out your fingertips.

» Continue moving down your legs, through your knees, and down your ankles. Pay attention to the sensations in your major joints: your ankles, knees, hips, wrists, elbows, and shoulders. If you feel the urge to move any of these, feel free to do so.

» Follow your attention into your feet, then down into your toes, then into bottoms of your feet.

> » Take a moment to notice where your soles meet the ground.
> » Notice the rising and falling of your chest as you breathe in and out.
> » When you are ready, open your eyes and come back to the room.

The Three As

Purpose: This practice lets each individual know that they are valued for both what they do and who they are as a person, which can help instill a feeling of physical safety.

Suggested Cadence: Once a month during a team meeting

At the beginning of a meeting, each individual in the meeting receives one appreciation, one acknowledgment, and one apology. These can come from three different people or all from one person.

> » An appreciation is something that a person did: "Thank you for responding so quickly to the customer's complaint."
> » An acknowledgment is who they are: "You are a very thoughtful person."
> » An apology is taking responsibility for a broken agreement: "I am sorry for being late to our meeting when I said I would be on time."

Boundaries

Purpose: This conversation allows everyone to gain clarity around one another's physical boundaries and to begin to create a shared work environment that feels inclusive to all bodies. Boundaries are defined as "what is ok and what is not ok" for any individual.

Suggested Cadence: Once a quarter, anytime there is a change to the immediate working team, anytime there is a change to the physical environment. (This may take several meetings depending on team size. Don't rush, try to fully hear and understand what each person is saying.)

Ask each individual on your immediate working team to make two lists:

> *List 1:* What is OK with me?
> *Example:* Having my camera on while I work at home
>
> *List 2:* What is not OK with me?
> *Example:* Meeting in a small, crowded room

Come together as a team and share your lists with one another. Commonalities across people can be made into team boundaries such as "We start meetings on time," while individual differences in boundaries need to be respected.

EMOTIONAL SAFETY

I define emotional safety as the shared belief that all emotions are valid and the expression of any emotion is welcome.

When I talk about this type of safety with leaders in an organization, I often get some pushback. Surely, you don't mean for people to share *any* emotion. What about lust? What about rage? We can't talk about those! That's going to get us in trouble with HR!

And yet, I do believe that it is not only appropriate but imperative to share any emotion at work. Human beings are emotional creatures, and when we suppress our feelings at work, we decrease our ability to effectively collaborate with others. Emotional safety maps to the mammalian part of our brain and directly impacts our ability to connect on a social level. A lack of emotional safety leads to feelings of tension, defensiveness, and irritability, all of which get in the way of people actually working together.

If you have ever been a part of a team in which morale was low, you would have experienced firsthand how productivity comes to a screeching halt because people don't feel good. Meetings become painful and bloated with all the emotions left unnamed.

If you are going through any kind of change or transformation process, the biggest obstacle to the change will be people's emotions. The reason 70 percent of change initiatives fail is because they don't guide people through the emotional stages of change toward acceptance, engagement, and even championing the change.

Furthermore, we have all experienced times when strong emotions have distorted our perceptions of a person or situation, and we "couldn't think straight." Well that is very literal because information has to pass through the mammalian part of our brain before it reaches our rational brain, directly impacting the thoughts we think. If we are scared, we are going to think about all the reasons against taking an action. If we are angry, we are going to think and focus on everything that is wrong in a situation. Emotions are lenses that can either distort our perceptions or help us see what is happening more clearly.

In my opinion, emotional safety is at the core of relating and relationships. How we relate to each other comes down to how we talk or don't talk about our emotions, and the ways we respond to each other's emotions. Do we have enough safety in our relationship that I can tell you I was offended by a comment that you made in the last meeting? Or hurt because you took credit for my idea? Or angry about being interrupted? Do I have confidence that you will react in a caring way? Or will I begin to find ways to avoid you, create workarounds, set up conditional ways of interacting, or withdraw because I don't feel safe sharing my emotions.

When we experience emotional safety, we feel internally relaxed around people. We have the freedom to let our guard down and be vulnerable with each other by sharing our hurts, fears, and longings. Emotional safety enables us to collaborate, listen, empathize, and connect, as well as to be creative, innovative, and bold in our thinking and ideas.

Unfortunately, most of us have never been taught how to validate, feel, and express our emotions in a way that strengthens our relationships.

So let's start by dispelling a common myth about emotions: that some emotions are positive and others are negative. This is factually incorrect. Emotions are a biochemical process that occurs in the body; they are literally energy in motion or e-motion. Thus, all emotions are valid because emotions are a process that is occurring inside a person's body, and this is not the same as a story that someone might have made up in their mind about why they are feeling a certain way.

According to Jill Bolte Taylor, Ph. D., the biochemical process lasts only 90 seconds. If an emotion lasts longer than 90 seconds, it's because we didn't attend to the emotion, setting off a series of thoughts and stories in our mind that create an emotional loop.

Many of us have experienced times in our life when we just couldn't stop thinking about a person or situation, the thoughts looping in our mind for hours. These thoughts restimulate the circuitry that results in the biochemical process occurring over and over again.

So, how does one attend to and feel emotions? By spending 90 seconds paying attention to the sensations we are experiencing in our body: a tightness in our stomach, a heaviness on our chest, heat on our arms or face, tingling on our fingers, tension in our shoulders, or even numbness.

Because emotions are a biochemical process that people can literally feel as sensations in the body, they are unarguable. Meaning, no one can argue that you are currently experiencing specific sensations in your body. And yet, the most common response in organizations when someone shares a feeling is to dismiss it by saying things such as "It's not that bad"; "You are overreacting"; "I'm sorry you feel that way"; "You shouldn't feel that way"; or "Don't think about it, just get over it."

In a culture of safety, people take the time—it takes only a few minutes really—to hear, validate, and understand one another's emotions. And when people feel safe to express their emotions, they can drop their armor, open up to each other, and know that they will be cared for regardless. This frees people up to attend to and move through their emotions in a healthy way, so they can have full access to their intelligence, focus, and creativity.

MEETING PRACTICES

The following meeting practices work to begin creating a culture in which people feel safe to feel and express their full range of their emotions.

Sensation Words

Purpose: This practice helps individuals tune into the way emotions show up in their body, allow them to feel the emotions, and express them to others in an unarguable way.

Suggested Cadence: Every day

Start using the four basic feeling words in daily conversation: *happy, angry, scared, sad.*

Add sensations words: *tight, heavy, tingling, tense, clenching, hot, cold, numb, fluttering, knotted, achy, trembling.*

Example: "When you were telling me about the plan for the next few months, I felt my stomach clench. I feel scared about this approach."

Check-in

Purpose: This practice allows people to emotionally connect to themselves and each other and creates an invitation for people to share emotions throughout the meeting.

Note: Sometimes after a check-in, the meeting facilitator will decide to change the agenda to meet the emotional state of the people in the room.

Suggested Cadence: Every team meeting

As part of meetings, go around the room and check in to see how each person is feeling. Ask for people to name both the feeling word and the sensation, with the facilitator of the meeting repeating back some of the themes they heard. For example: "It seems we have a mix of emotions in the room. Some folks are feeling sad while others are feeling scared."

If you want to take this one step further, you can create an emotion dashboard for each team meeting on which people place icons and words to describe their current emotional state. As a leader, an aggregate view of these check-ins over several months can help you visualize the morale of the team or hone in on an individual that may be struggling emotionally.

Over time, having regular check-ins will help people build the awareness of their body and in turn their emotions, creating emotional safety.

Venting Session

Purpose: This session gives people the opportunity to express their feelings while being heard and validated. Creating a space and time for people to vent reduces gossip and backbiting within a team.

Suggested Cadence: Once a month in a one-on-one or team meeting, anytime there is a change, or a dip in morale

Specifically let people know that you are holding a "venting session," so they understand that this is the designated time for this type of conversation.

» Ask people to start complaining about anything that they don't like on the team. Timebox the complaining from five to 20 minutes depending on the group size.

» As people are complaining, listen for what they care about or what is important to them.

» Once they are done complaining, say, "Thank you. I heard that you care about ... and ... is important to you ... Is that correct?"

» They might say that is not correct and vent or add a bit more. Continue to listen for what they care about and repeat it back to them once again.

» Stay away from repeating any of their actual complaints; just focus on listening for what is behind the complaint.

PSYCHOLOGICAL SAFETY

Amy Edmondson, Ph. D., of the Harvard Business School, defines psychological safety as the shared belief that no one on the team will embarrass or punish anyone else for admitting a mistake, asking a question, or offering a new idea.

In a 2016 study conducted by Google on what makes an effective team, the researchers identified psychology safety as the number-one factor impacting team effectiveness. They noticed that when it came to team effectiveness, it mattered less who was on the team and more on how they worked together. Psychological safety maps to the rational part of our brain, and directly impacts our ability to first come up with new ideas and then have the willingness to share them with others.

A lack of psychological safety creates one of the biggest threats to business health and longevity: silence.

Several studies show that silence is painfully common, and that people stay silent even when they believe that what they have to say could be important for the organization, the customer, or themselves. The result? Problems go unreported, opportunities for innovation are missed, and occasionally, tragic failures occur that could have been avoided.

Why do people stay silent? Fear. Fear of being viewed or judged negatively, and fear of damaging work relationships.

In her research, Edmonson found a small set of common fear-based beliefs that govern when people choose to remain silent. They are essentially beliefs about when it is and isn't appropriate to speak to higher-ups in an organization. The beliefs include:

> » Don't criticize something the boss may have helped create.
> » Don't speak unless you have solid data.
> » Don't speak up if the boss' boss is present.
> » Don't speak up in a group with anything negative about the work to prevent the boss from losing face.

These beliefs make it harder to achieve innovation.

Although it's often difficult to measure innovations that didn't happen as a result of low psychological safety, we can see the impact by the rise and fall of companies over the years. Take Nokia for example: In the late 1990s, Nokia was the world's leading mobile phone manufacturer, but by 2012, the company's share of the smartphone market had dropped by over 75 percent. An in-depth investigation of Nokia's rise and fall, which included 76 managers and engineers, concluded that the company lost the smartphone battle not as a result of poor vision or a few bad managers but at least partly due to a "fearful emotional climate" that created company-wide inertia. When middle managers asked critical questions about the company's direction, they were told to "focus on implementation." People who could not comply with top managers unreasonable requests were "labeled a loser." Senior managers even reported that "it was very difficult to tell [the CEO] things he didn't want to hear." Nokia has not been able to recover market share to this day.

Aside from innovation, an environment of psychological safety allows people to speak up about mistakes that occurred, as well as help one another course correct to avoid potentially costly mistakes. Imagine the potential cost savings that would be available in your organization if people spent less energy on covering up mistakes, and more time helping one another solve the underlying problems.

Finally, it's important to mention that psychological safety isn't the result of being nice. Quite the opposite, actually. Edmondson says that psychological safety is about candor and a certain level of healthy conflict in the workplace. When managers and employees inauthentically support one another's ideas in the name of being polite, they miss out on an opportunity to learn. On the other hand, people who know that their voices are being heard, that their opinions are valued and even occasionally challenged by the team, will feel empowered to take action and innovate.

MEETING PRACTICES

The following meeting practices work to begin creating a culture in which people feel safe to speak up by sharing ideas, asking questions, and admitting mistakes.

High Dream–Low Dream

Purpose: This meeting encourages people to share their thoughts with each other and higher-ups by providing an opportunity to be heard without repercussions or jumping to solutions.

Suggested Cadence: Every project or initiative kickoff

Using a whiteboard, create two columns and label them "Hopes" and "Concerns." Ask each team member to write their highest hopes and biggest concerns for the project in the appropriate columns.

After everyone has put up their thoughts, discuss people's hopes first and then their concerns second. As the leader, make sure everyone has a chance to speak. Point out themes that you see in both the hopes and concerns, but don't jump in and try to fix the concerns. Instead, allow the team to find their own way by asking, "How can we ensure that we reach our hopes and minimize our concerns?"

Mistake Celebration

Purpose: This meeting creates an environment in which everyone feels safe to admit and learn from mistakes.

Suggested Cadence: Once a month

Hold a special meeting celebrating mistakes and lessons learned this month. Make this meeting fun and light-hearted, perhaps even giving away prizes for the biggest lessons learned. It's important for leaders to always go first and admit their mistakes to model that it is OK to speak up about mistakes.

Sparring

Purpose: This practice helps people learn how to have productive conflict that leads to new and innovative ideas. It's also a good chance to invite members outside of your team or discipline to be able to take advantage of their expertise.

Suggested Cadence: During the strategy or ideation stage of a project or initiative

Think carefully about what topic or idea you would like to bring to the sparring session. Be sure to send out any pre-work when you invite people to the session so they can be prepared for the discussion. Timebox each sparring session for a maximum of 30 minutes.

At the start of the session, briefly present your topic or idea to set the context. Give just enough information to get oriented but don't explain anything just yet.

Invite the team to challenge you and find the weak spots in your topic or idea. Your team can challenge you on why you are doing this, details of what you are doing, and how you are doing it. Challenging leadership or each other can lead to feelings of vulnerability and discomfort, but encourage it anyway. When people are willing to step outside of their comfort zone and speak up, the idea can evolve into something truly innovative.

When you are receiving challenges, spend more time getting curious and fully understanding the thinking behind the challenge then justifying or defending your idea.

Capture any outstanding questions or issues, and schedule a follow-up sparring session if necessary. Make it clear what you will do with the information that came out of the session.

CHAPTER 6: FINAL THOUGHTS

At the end of the day, a culture of safety is about our connections to one another as human beings.

As Brené Brown poignantly states: "Connection is why we're here. We are hardwired to connect with others; it's what gives purpose and meaning to our lives, and without it there is suffering."

I know that I, along with millions of others, have suffered in silence at work. My hope is that the practices in this book will help create cultures of safety in which everybody is valued, validated, and heard. This is how we are going to bring out the best in each other, our teams, and organizations.

It's scary to embark on the journey of creating a culture of safety. And it's much easier to live with the cultures we know—where self-protection drowns out creativity and belonging—rather than a culture of safety that we don't know, with unusual meeting practices that invite candor, vulnerability, and even conflict.

And so, I invite you to courage. To feel the fear and set sail anyway... on a journey to create an environment in which people can think, collaborate, and innovate.

After all, as author John Augustus Shedd said: "A ship is safe in a harbor, but that's not what ships are made for."

READING LIST

All the practices and tools mentioned in this book,
plus many more, can be downloaded as handouts at:
http://www.spokeandwheel.co/learn-with-us.

Brown, Brené. *Dare to Lead: Brave Work, Tough Conversations, Whole Hearts.* Random House, 2018.

Chapman, Bob. "A Most Momentous Day," 5 Oct. 2015, https://www.trulyhumanleadership.com/?p=2517

Edmondson, Amy. "Boeing and the Importance of Encouraging Employees to Speak Up." *Harvard Business Review*, last updated 4 May 2019, www.hbr.org/2019/05/boeing-and-the-importance -of-encouraging-employees-to-speak-up.

Edmonson, Amy. *The Fearless Organization: Creating Psychological Safety in the Workplace for Learning, Innovation, and Growth.* John Wiley & Sons, 2019.

The Official Site of the Karpman Triangle: https://karpmandramatriangle.com/.

Laloux, Frederic, and Ken Wilber. *Reinventing Organizations: A Guide to Creating Organizations Inspired By the Next Stage in Human Consciousness.* Nelson Parker, 2014.

Menakem, Resmaa. *My Grandmother's Hands: Healing Racial Trauma in Our Minds and Bodies.* Penguin Books, 2021.

McLaren, Karla. "Fear: Intuition, Instincts, and Awareness." 21 June 2013, https://karlamclaren.com/fear-intuition -instincts-and-awareness/.

Snowden, David J., and Mary E. Boone. "A Leader's Framework for Decision Making." *Harvard Business Review*, Nov. 2007, www.hbr.org/2007/11/a-leaders-framework-for-decision-making.

"Understanding the Stress Response." Harvard Health Publishing, last updated 6 July 2020, www.health.harvard.edu/staying-healthy/understanding-the-stress-response.

Wehmiller, Barry. "Guiding Principles of Leadership," https://www.barrywehmiller.com/docs/default-source/barrywehmiller-vision-documents/guiding-principles-of-leadership.pdf.

ALLA WEINBERG specializes in helping companies build cultures where people feel safe, respected, and able to do their best work.

She is a workplace relationships expert and the CEO of Spoke & Wheel, a people and team development company. Alla builds loving leaders, trusting teams, and cultures of safety through training, coaching, and facilitation.

www.spokeandwheel.co
in allaweinberg

Printed in Great Britain
by Amazon

25914607R00040